Restore Order. Restore Joy.

Happy Organizing!
Dorothy

Restore Order. Restore Joy.

How To Get Your Life in Order After a Loss

Dorothy L. Clear, CPO

ISBN-13: 9780692761977
ISBN-10: 0692761977

Restore Order.
Restore Joy.

What People Are Saying

"A wonderful storyteller, Dorothy shares her personal experiences to explain how "life" impacts one's perspective around stuff. She then delivers solid, practical, and concrete advice on what to do to move on and change your relationship with your things so that you can restore order and joy to your life. Dorothy gives you hope!"

Ellen Faye COC®, CPO®, President, National Association of Professional Organizers (NAPO)

"Restore Order. Restore Joy." sends a powerful message to those who live with clutter, depression, anxiety, addiction or grief – it's perfectly acceptable to ask for and receive help. Dorothy Clear courageously shares her story to let her readers know they are not alone and her commitment to continue working with others in need is unwavering. Dorothy's understanding and tools make this book a pure outpouring of inspiration!"

Patty Kreamer, CPO®
Author of "...But I Might Need It Someday", "The Power of Simplicity", and co-author of "Success Simplified"

"Restore Order. Restore Joy - How to Get Your Life in Order After a Loss" by Dorothy Clear uses her personal experiences throughout the book to help people who have clutter due to the loss of a loved one. As a professional organizer she has been able to apply her life experiences with her own losses to help clients who are experiencing their own loss to help them through the de-cluttering and organizing process. She gives a plan to her reader on how to get organized, and provides encouragement along the way. A nice guide for people who have experienced grief and loss and are disorganized and don't know where to start. Dorothy's book can help you!"

Vickie Dellaquila, CPO®, CPO-CD®
Author of *"Don't Toss My Memories in the Trash-A Step-by-Step Guide to Helping Seniors Downsize, Organize, and Move"*

This book is dedicated to my late father, Steve A. Cuban.
Oct. 2, 1935 – June 3, 1994

God's Garden
Unknown

God Looked Around His Garden
And Found an Empty Place.
And Saw Your Tired Face.
He Put His Arms Around You
And Lifted You To Rest.
God's Garden Must Be Beautiful
He Always Takes The Best
He Knows That You Were Suffering
He Knew That You Were In Pain
He Knew That You Would Never
Get Well On Earth Again.
He Saw The Road Was Getting Rough
And The Hills Were Hard To Climb.
So He Closed Your Weary Eyelids,
And Whispered "PEACE BE THINE".
It Broke Our Hearts To Lose You
But You Don't Go Alone
For Part Of Us Went With You
The Day God Called You Home.

Contents

Acknowledgments

A loving God, as I understand Him.

Nancy Cuban – The strongest, most loving mother (grandmother and great grandmother) in the world. I am so grateful for our relationship.

Arthur F. Clear - My funny, sweet, gentle, stubborn, rebellious, worrisome husband who loves me for who I am, flaws and all. And, I love him flaws and all. We believe God was our matchmaker. Your support means the world to me.

Stephanie Scanlon – My BIG sister who inspires me with her strengths and her weaknesses.

Lora Holtz – My younger sister who gave me a suggestion that changed my life.

Chad Cuban – My son…the best creation I have ever made.

Connie Egan, Bunny Pittsburgh, Karen Allen, Rossann Ponce, Patricia Joseph, Jennifer Belobrajdic Baumann, Jennifer Smith, Dubravka Bencic, Belinda Hayes, Jessica Fondy, and the late Paula B. Hill for your friendship over the years.

A very special thank you to a dear friend Missie Burford. She asked me for a favor and it changed my life.

The National Association of Professional Organizers Pittsburgh Chapter members; especially my accountability partner Shawndra Holmberg.

Julie Morgenstern, Matt Paxton, and Dr. Suzanne Chabaud, Dr. Randy Frost, Dr. David Tolin and Dr. Gail Steketee for being my mentors, educators, and inspiration.

Sarah Lewis – A Guiding Force brought me to this gentle, handsome women; first as a client, then as my book editor, and now I call her my friend.

Preface

*Having anxiety and depression is like being scared
and tired at the same time. It's the fear of failure but
no urge to be productive. It's wanting friends but,
hating to socialize. It's wanting to be alone but not
wanting to be lonely. It's caring about everything
then caring about nothing. Its feeling everything
at once then feeling paralyzing numbness.*

AUTHOR UNKNOWN

⤴

Fear knocked at the door.
Faith answered, and no one was there.

AUTHOR UNKNOWN

Who is this book for?

- Anyone who has clutter the state of which can be traced back to a traumatic event or loss. Examples may include loss of a job or retirement which caused you to be unsure of your identity. The death of a loved one. The loss of health or mobility. Those suffering from depression.
- People who work with those who have grief and depression, so they can better understand how collecting, acquiring, clutter and hoarding may manifest itself in some people.

Introduction

As our nation ages we see more and more people needing help with their stuff and it takes a specific voice to help one realize it's time for a change. Dorothy Clear and her new book "Restore Order. Restore Joy." might be that unique voice that just might help you make a change. I've personally worked side by side with Dorothy Clear on some of the most challenging hoarded homes in the country and can't wait to see how she and her book help you get your life back.

Matt Paxton, Extreme Cleaning Specialist
Author of "The Secret Lives of Hoarders"
Co-Executive Producer of the documentary, "Out of Luck"

Definition of a professional organizer:

The difference became very clear when I mentored other organizers starting out. I've had so many people over the years say "if you ever need help, I'm super organized". Yes but applying true organizing principles to achieve your clients' desired outcome, not yours, every time is what makes you a professional. You have to listen, truly listen to the client and solve the unique problems they have in a way that makes sense to them. You have to put all judgement aside and become whatever they need to get them through the process; psychologist, marriage counsellor, confidant, teacher, coach, etc. You have to be willing to listen to subtle clues, recognize nuances and shift gears accordingly when you've touched a nerve. You need to know when to push and when to back off. In my experience, very few people can do this job well of those reasons. I'm sure many of you have heard horror stories from clients hiring the wrong "professional organizer" before you who simply wanted to back a waste bin up to the house and dump everything of the clients into it!! Anyone can learn to be organized but to be a professional you have to innately have these qualities then spend time honing them as you gain experience. The clients' needs are the focus, not you or your agenda. You are simply the guide in their process.

Karen Scaddan
Certified Professional Organizer
Get Organized Windsor
www.getorganizedwindsor.com
Windsor, ON, Canada

One

MY STORY

June 3, 1994 started out like any other day. I got showered, styled my hair, put on my dress clothes and took the bus to my office job in downtown Pittsburgh. I was the Safety Administrator for a major chain of department stores. Our back office consisted of me and my boss, the Safety Director. I had been in the position since October the year before. I had transferred from the Human Resources Department at our warehouse where I worked for three years.

That morning was ordinary. And then, I got a phone call from my mother. My dad had died in his bed overnight. My dad was fifty-eight years old. He just died.

I broke down crying and felt I could not stop.

But, I did stop, temporarily, to get home. I walked a few blocks to the nearest hotel and got a cab. During the cab ride my world seemed to stop. But the world outside the cab kept going...traffic, pedestrians. None of it mattered. I felt numb.

I went straight to my dad's house. I had to see him. I hugged my mom, then walked up stairs to see him lying in bed.

I have always been calm under pressure. Able to handle emergency situations without panic. But this; this shook my world. I thought I was handling my grief well. In the following days I continued to function as wife, mother, daughter, employee, sister, lector at my church, executor of my dad's estate. But, something shifted inside me. When I was not busy and had time to myself, the grief was overwhelming. The pain of that loss was too great to handle.

I stopped crying temporarily. I don't mean that day. The crying would last for two years as my drinking would escalate.

And, my dad didn't just die. While maybe he did, according to the doctors. We did not have an autopsy. But, in their opinion, since he was not suffering from any acute life threatening illness it was probably a cardiac episode. However, it is important to my story to tell you my dad had degenerative arthritis, gastritis, depression and alcoholism. And, he smoked unfiltered cigarettes most of his life. He also had control issues which could lead to rage, or he would stop talking to you completely. I remember as an adolescent being yelled at for sitting on his shirt which was hanging on the back of the chair. And, if you made him angry, he could stay angry for years.

I cut a phone conversation with him short one time and he quit talking to me for four years. It was during the planning of my first wedding, which he did not attend. I walked down the aisle by myself. I tried numerous times to reconcile with him, but he wouldn't have it. Then one day I was walking home with groceries and he and my younger sister were driving by. They offered me a ride and we were on speaking terms again.

It's also important to say I both loved and hated my dad.

When my dad died I had many mixed emotions. He worked hard to provide for his family; sometimes, he held down two jobs. He and my mom paid for me and my two sisters to attend Catholic school. We had a clean home. He worked on his car and in his basement work shop. He was very smart and was always doing crossword puzzles, drawing cartoons, writing poems, doing small wood sculptures. He was very generous and would buy me and my sisters anything we needed, or wanted, within reason. As adults, he would help us out financially if we were late paying a bill or needed something for our children.

Here is a poem he wrote about my name dated July 19, 1980 which he gave to me. Incidentally, I was named after one of his sisters, my late Aunt Dorothy, whom he loved dearly. And, he gave this to me five months after I gave birth to his first grandchild. It is typed here exactly as he wrote it. I still have the paper he hand wrote. He was practicing his calligraphy at that time.

What a lovely name, Dorothy,
it sounds so light and free.
It dances on the very air,
it pictures, not a care.
What a solid name, Dorothy,
she stands as an oak tree.
Someone, in whom to place a trust,
she will endure, till the arena turns to rust.

What a happy name, Dorothy,
Just like a classic comedy.
And when her voice you hear,
it fills you full of cheer.

Yes, a godly name Dorothy,
she can lift you spiritually,
so delicate and yet so strong,
You know, she will do no wrong.

Oh, such a grand name, Dorothy,
She will see you over your tragedy,
and chase away all the gloom,
bringing sunshine into the room.

And it's Cora, the Coffee Lady's real name,
playing in the movies, her fame,
she played the Wicked witch of the West,
in the "Wizard of Oz", and she melted the best.

s a Cuban
7-19-80

But, he could be very contradictory or spiteful.

Take his will for instance. He had been trying for months to get me and my sisters to sit down with him to help him write out his will. Either we could not find the time or we found it too morbid. The point is he couldn't do it his way. When he died we were lucky enough to find a sealed, unmarked envelope. Inside was a handwritten note on a small piece of paper folded in thirds. It was dated April fool's day of that year (2 months before he died), and he did not sign his name, he printed it. He left everything to me and one of his grandchildren, and cut everyone else out. We could have easily missed it among his papers. And, it was not legally binding anyway because it didn't have his signature. My sisters and I agreed to follow what he had written. However, as executor of his estate I shared my portion of the insurance with them and my mom. Everyone got what they needed.

When he drank, he had a different side. His personality changed. He became belligerent, argumentative, verbally abusive, and occasionally even physically abusive to my mom. I cannot recount how many times my mom had dinner waiting on the table for my dad to come home from the steel mill. We kids would be starving from playing outside after school. But, he would be a no show because he stopped at the bar on the way home. Or, maybe he wrecked his car, which happened on more than one occasion; or, got a DWI (driving while intoxicated). That also happened frequently. This predated MADD, *Mothers Against Drunk Drivers,* and the stiffer laws and penalties.

There were at least three stays at a detox center and/or inpatient rehab. I had to 302 him once. That's when you sign a person into the hospital for a 72 hour hold because they are a threat to themselves or someone else. I believe there were 6 DWIs. I remember at least 3 wrecked cars, and 2 trips to jail. I called the police once because he had my mom pinned to the living room floor and was pulling her hair. He was furious. I was full of shame because the neighbors all came out to see the show.

One day, after my parents had separated, my dad came to the house for some reason. They were arguing. He was saying really hateful, cruel, and nasty things to my mom. Somehow, I got the courage to stand up to him. I told him not to talk to my mother that way. "This isn't your house". I told him to leave, he told me to stay out of it or he would put me through a wall. I was 15 years old.

I grew up in fear, shame, humiliation, and, strangely enough, LOVE. We knew he loved us. But, he was the proverbial Dr. Jekyll and Mr. Hyde. I had a tremendous amount of love for my father and an equal amount of resentments.

So, when he died I was sorrowful but relieved. I didn't know if he would go to heaven. I missed talking to him, getting his advice on a problem at work or sharing good news with him. He either smelled of Brut cologne or Old Spice; or, he smelled of cigarettes and beer. I missed that too. If you have ever lost someone close to you, you probably remember in that first year receiving good news and wanting to share it with them. Only to remember that you can't. Or, walking somewhere and smelling their cologne or perfume, and looking around to see if they are there. Or, seeing someone from a distance and thinking that it's your loved one, only to feel that lose again.

What I didn't miss were the rude voice mails he would leave on my answering machine. I didn't always take his drunken calls. Or, when I would go visit and he would ask me to go to the corner bar and get him a six-pack. Not because he couldn't do it himself; but, because he had caused trouble there and was asked not to come back. He was barred.

When I was thirty-three, I had so many resentments that had nothing to do with my father because my own life was falling apart. I was unhappy in my job, my marriage and I felt stuck in my life. It was the perfect run way for my alcoholism to take off and soar. My drinking was out of control for the next two years.

I cried and drank, and cried and drank. I tried counseling for my emotions, but she wanted to examine my drinking. I never went back.

In March 1995, I ended my 12-year marriage and moved. I used my dad's inheritance to get us out of debt. I quit attending church and was dating an atheist. I barely saw my teenage son. I lost my job in December. I tried counseling again, but it didn't work because I was still drinking. I didn't know if I should celebrate Christmas because I didn't know what I believed in any more. It got so bad that in May 1996 I totaled the car my dad left me. I went into outpatient rehab. I have been sober ever since.

Now, imagine that instead of my drinking to medicate all those uncomfortable feelings of grief and resentment I started uncontrollable shopping or collecting. And, I didn't pick up after myself or throw anything away. Or, I started overeating to mask those feelings. Or, exercised and starved myself. Or, slept around. Or, cut myself.

My point is that clutter and hoarding can result from unresolved grief or depression. I include depression too because it has extremely close characteristics to grief. And, my story and the stories of many of my clients involve both.

I never wanted to be alcoholic. I've overcome a lot by the Grace of God. I was often teased by kids when I was growing up. I was a bit of an ugly duckling from fifth grade until my sophomore year of high school. I have a turned up nose. I had trouble saying my R's. I was tall (still am) and very thin, I wore glasses, my hair had no body or volume. You get the idea. Things turned around for me as I grew into myself. Our grade school had me in speech therapy. During adolescence I developed a shape, and in high school I got contact lenses.

However, there was constant criticism and emotional manipulation by my dad, and fear of what would happen next in our house. It explains why I was so fearful, self-conscious and insecure.

I constantly talked to myself in a negative voice and sabotaged my own efforts. Through the help of others I have been able to recover from my childhood traumas and lack of coping skills.

Throughout this book I will share the philosophies I have used in my life to achieve personal growth and become accountable for my own actions.

Philosophy #1: If you don't talk to yourself with respect, how can you expect anyone else to?

In college, I sought counseling for abandonment issues when my best friend moved out of state. It brought out feelings I was harboring from my dad leaving after the divorce, and the father of my child rejecting us. I attended grief counseling after my dad died. I went to outpatient rehab for my drinking problem. Three years after I stopped drinking I was diagnosed with depression, which I suffered with my entire life, and started taking an antidepressant. The faith I lost due to my drinking has been restored. I am comfortable in my own skin. I am happy with the woman I am today. But, I didn't do it alone. I have learned that if I need help...*I need to ask for it.* When I have humbly asked for help it has changed your life.

Not only is success about asking for help, it requires taking the leap of faith, taking action or doing something different and new. I have been afraid of loads of things but I have done them anyway. And, it has made me emotionally stronger in the long run.

Many of my dreams have come true because I have been shown how to set goals and work toward them. I have developed coping skills for dealing with anger, shame, depression, fear and resentment. I have learned to follow direction.

Philosophy #2: Walk through your fear.

I am not a therapist, but I have a tremendous reserve of empathy, compassion and understanding for others. Because of my past, I believe I can help empower my clients to overcome the obstacles holding them back from living the life they want. I'll even walk part of that path with them.

I want to use my experiences and "super powers" of observation and organization to help others who have accumulated clutter due to their grief or depression because I understand these life situations. I've lived through them. And, due to the help I have received along the way, I am a stronger person and can help others get through their issues too.

Philosophy #3: Anything is possible if you put your mind to it.

Two

How I Got Here

Surround yourself with the dreamers and the doers, the believers and thinkers, but most of all, surround yourself with those who see greatness within you, even when you don't see it yourself.

— Healing Light

People ask me how I got started as a Professional Organizer. I usually start the story with, "In 2011 I was unemployed and an acquaintance asked me to help her de-clutter her house". But, let's go back *a little bit* further.

In the summer of 1998, I was between jobs and a woman that I knew asked me to help her clear out and organize her basement. She couldn't do it by herself because of crippling arthritis in her thumbs. She was willing to pay me a small hourly amount. I agreed and I liked doing it. I really liked her company and we became friends.

When we finished the basement, she asked me to be her personal assistant. She was amazed at my packing skills; technical term "spatial relations".

I helped two more friends clean out their basements as favors. I never imaged I was training for a future career. I have always helped family and friends move.

In May 2007, my mother lost the love of her life, my step-father. They had been together 25 years. He lost his battle with emphysema and lung cancer. One year after he passed away, she had to downsize and moved in with my younger sister. The family helped her move.

In August 2007, I got remarried. Then, in February 2008, my new father-in-law passed away. He lost his battle with ALS and lung cancer. My new mother-in-law had to downsize and move a year after his death. Again, the family helped her move.

Then a woman I knew who, like me was also trying to get sober, asked me to help her clean up her townhouse. For the last few years she had only been going there to drink. Most of the time she stayed with her boyfriend. The neighbors were complaining and she might lose her house. Her place was deplorable like you see on the evening news…garbage everywhere, clothes, dust, bottles, cans, bugs. My husband and I helped her shovel stuff into garbage bags.

Then, the advent of reality TV hit the scene with shows like *Hoarders, Clean Sweep, Design on a Dime, What Not to Wear*, etc. I loved them! Well, I didn't love Hoarders. I found that show hard to watch, but very interesting. I felt sorry for those people. I thought of it as another out of control addiction. My husband and I resolved to never let that happen to us!

Then, in December 2010, I was fired from my corporate human resources job, which was crazy, because I had just been promoted in May under a different manager. But, there was a turnover in management. So, out with the old, in with the new. I thought…UGH! What am I going to do? I was forty-nine years old, was three years into a new marriage with two stepchildren, living in a new town, we just bought a house in June, and I had to start looking for a new job!? This isn't fair!!!

Philosophy #4: Sometimes things happen for a reason.

The company I had worked for was a mortgage services company. When we bought our house that June, we saved money on the closing costs since I was an employee. And, now that I was home during the day, I could fulfill one of my husband's dreams. He had always wanted to own an English bulldog. So, we adopted Gus.

Three years before this I had learned how to ride a motorcycle and was still riding my 1996 Honda Rebel 250cc. But guess what? It was time for a big girl bike. I moved up to a 2006 Honda Shadow VLX600. Gosh…I didn't know what I was missing!!! I love the power of my bigger bike.

I turned 50 years old in May 2011 and went skydiving for the first time. It was the thrill of a lifetime!!!

All this time, I was going through the motions of job hunting. And, praying. Every day I prayed that I would know God's will for my life.

I have always had an entrepreneurial spirit. And, my parents instilled in me a great work ethic. When I was a child, we would help neighbors carry their groceries home for spare change. We would collect soda pop bottles, return them to the store and collect the five cents return. I walked in the March of Dimes walkathons to raise money for the charity. I held a back yard fair to raise money for Jerry's Kids (MS, Muscular Dystrophy). I dusted shelves at the local pharmacy where my mother worked to earn money to buy my own shoes and clothes.

Then in high school, I sold yearbook boosters. I also tried waitressing at the neighborhood diner. I was an absolute disaster in that job, and lasted a week or two. In my senior year I worked part-time in the dietary department of a local hospital.

I put myself through 4-years of college starting at the age of 23, one week after I recovered from a collapsed lung. Although I started a week behind every other student, I caught up. The second semester I made the dean's list. After graduation I pursued a career in human resources. I was good at that career and let it define me. I specialized in recruitment, benefits, safety and worker compensation. I held positions with titles such as HR rep, employment specialist, HR generalist, benefits administrator.

But, I dreamed of more. Why didn't I have a special talent? I wondered if I could own my own business someday. I've always wished I could invent something that would make me rich and/or impact the world.

On occasion, I found myself between jobs. Every time I would have this same internal struggle. Is there something more, or something else, I could be doing. Could I be a consultant? Be my own boss?

In the past, I had a few failed ideas which I worked on but they never materialized into much. Once upon a time I was going to market my ex-husband's salsa recipe. I had a direct sales business for a while. And, I took a correspondence course in an attempt to become a florist. I wrote a business plan and applied for a loan to open a flower shop. The loan was denied because of my credit score.

Philosophy #5: Unanswered prayers (or failures) can be a blessing in disguise.

Then in July 2011, a friend asked me to help her de-clutter her house. I honestly don't even remember how it came up in conversation. But, we talked about it and I agreed to do it for a small hourly fee. I told her I had thought about doing this as a career, and this would give me the opportunity to see if I like doing it, and if I am any good at it. In the meantime, I started researching the industry. *I HAD FOUND MY PASSION!*

I did some market research to see if this idea was viable in my area. I created a survey on Survey Monkey and sent it out to all my contacts. In conversation with friends I asked if they would hire someone to help them organize and how much they would be willing to spend. I discussed it with my husband. At first he was not really supportive of the idea.

My husband has always been a blue collar guy. What they call a "man's man", like my dad and my husband's father. He works in a trade, works forty hours a week plus overtime, and brings home a pay check. I was like that most of my adult life, also. It scared him that I would want to give up the comfortable salary of my corporate world to claw and scratch out my own living wage. But, he also knew the toll the stress of my corporate job was having on me physically. So, he reluctantly supported the idea. But, he also encouraged me to find a part-time job.

During this research phase, I bought a book written by Dawn Noble entitled "<u>How to Start a Home-based Professional Organizing Business</u>". I almost wept while reading the acknowledgments and introduction.

Acknowledgments excerpt: *To my husband Chris: Always the biggest thank you goes to you. Your patience, grace, and simple way of taming my crazy astounds me. During a recent episode of crazy…. you simply kissed my forehead and said, "I knew what I was getting into when I said "I Do".*

Introduction excerpt: "*As my husband walked out the door for his yearly golf adventure in the Carolinas, I told him that by the time he returned I would have made a decision about my career. This* *came after a year of self-imposed unemployment, due to my decision to leave a nursing job that was financially rewarding but emotionally exhausting-so demanding that it took a toll on my health. My husband gone, the house quiet, I was now alone with my thoughts.*

How was I going to create a work life that was everything I wanted it to be? And what was it that I wanted, anyway? I went for a drive, the questions racing through my head. What would I love to do tomorrow? Could lose track of time doing? And wouldn't care if someone paid me or not? The answer: Clean out a closet.

The minute my husband arrived home, I rushed to him and said, 'I'll be cleaning out closets for a living!' He smiled and said, "I don't get it, but if it makes you happy, go for it."

Although that was not the same experience I had with my husband, because he did not think anyone would pay me help them organize, it was the experience I wanted. And, he will often say, "I know what I signed up for when I married you."

In the last few years my husband has seen the depth of my work as a Professional Organizer and has become my biggest supporter. He keeps his eyes open for opportunities for me, he carries one of my business cards with him in case he can hand it to someone. He has let me borrow his truck so I can help a client by taking their unwanted items to the donation center. And, he doesn't let anyone drive his truck!!!

I have to occasionally remind him of the advantages: more time to manage our home, to be there for our last teen at home and care for our two dogs. And, I'm happier, healthier and have less stress. I'm living my dream, fulfilling a passion, and helping others.

The next thing I found in my research was the National Association of Professional Organizers (NAPO). As soon as I could afford the membership fee I joined. This gave me credibility in my new vocation.

I attended their annual conference the following April. I convinced my husband to let me use some of our income tax refund for the registration fee and hotel cost. That year the conference was in Baltimore so I could drive which would cut down on costs. While I was there I met many of the members of our NAPO Pittsburgh Chapter. This group made me feel welcomed and enthusiastically invited me to their next monthly chapter meeting as a guest. I fell in love with these women and our chapter. Here was the support I needed. I did attend their May meeting. I joined immediately. And, since they had a vacant position on their board of directors, I volunteered to be their Marketing Director. I held that position for two years and it opened up so many opportunities for me. It gave me a chance to talk to professional organizers who have been working in the field for ten plus years to see how they got started, if I was on track with my business, and gain momentum and motivation to keep trying. I made contacts in print media and local libraries, I learned how to write a press release, and I organized a fundraiser and a community project. My new colleagues wrote recommendations on my LinkedIn page; LinkedIn is a business-oriented social networking service. That meant so much to me.

I also served as their board Secretary, and I have been elected for a second year as their President (2015-2017). This group has been instrumental in my growth as a professional organizer, business women, leader, and as a human being.

We have attended conferences together, solved problems for each other, and as a group we have improved our chapter, shared resources, socialized outside our meetings, supported each other through death and divorce, passed on referrals, hired each other as independent contractors, and trained the next person to take over our board positions.

I have a tremendously supportive team to turn to when I am in need. All of this validates me and my new profession.

Philosophy #6: Build relationships with people whom you can help and who can help you.

There are many things I can't do on my own. But "<u>We</u>" can do anything together. Build your "<u>We</u>".

Three

WHY I HELP OTHERS

*Give what you have. To someone, it may
be better than you dare to think.*

— HENRY WADSWORTH LONGFELLOW

This is why I help others. This is why I believe that, for me, being a professional organizer is more than just a profession; it's more of a vocation.

I know I did not get to where I am today by myself. Many people have helped me along the way. I have always participated in fundraisers walk-a-thons, 5K runs, selling gift wrap, collecting shoes, donating money or canned goods, because sometimes people need a helping hand.

I have been on welfare. I have been to a food pantry. I have been in debt and needed to borrow money. When I was depressed I sought counseling. When I got sober, other sober women taught me how to live a sober life. It is important to me to give back what I have been given…to pay it forward.

Philosophy #7: There, but for the Grace of God, go I.

Sharing your specific struggle with someone can help them overcome the same struggle. That's why support groups are successful in helping people with alcoholism, narcotic drug use, gambling, debt and disease. It doesn't matter if your problem is cancer, clutter or grief. There is a support group out there where you can find like-minded people who are going through what you are going through, where you can talk about your problem and get hope to get through it or live with it. You will find acceptance and hope for a brighter future.

If it makes you feel uncomfortable asking for help, consider it a resource to learn or try something new to solve your clutter or collecting problem. Or, consider this; the 12th Step in any 12-Step recovery program is to continue working with others... *"Carry the message to the still suffering (fill in the blank)"*. Once you have recovered, you are uniquely qualified to help others the way you have been helped.

The point is, you have to face the past in order to heal from it. Whether that is in a support group or with a private therapist, you will benefit from talking to others.

So, this is what I have learned. When I make the decision to work on myself and my problem(s), I then have to take the necessary steps to overcome my problem in order to succeed in moving past it. Then, I will be able to help others by sharing the solutions I have found that worked.

The biggest obstacle I have had is my own pride. Making an investment in my personal growth means admitting I have a problem and asking for help. From my own experiences working with others, I can tell you that far too many people cannot humble themselves to get the help they need. Or, they have fear of the unknown which is paralyzing. In extreme cases, it can lead to death: the middle aged man who dies from alcoholism at the age of fifty-eight; a teenager who dies of an overdose of heroin; the gambler $100,000 in debt, the veteran with untreated PTSD that commits suicide; the hoarder buried when the hoard falls on them. Or, their home catches fire and they can't get out, and firefighters can't get in.

My stepfather, for whatever reason, hated going to the doctor or dentist. Therefore, he did not go for regular checkups. He only went if he was in extreme pain, or tired of my mother's prodding him. That's why his lung cancer wasn't detected early. And, then he delayed the start of cancer treatment. His cancer was complicated due to emphysema because he was a lifelong smoker and due to chemicals used in his job in an auto body shop. And, he was a daily drinker.

The tumor was inoperable, so they did chemo and radiation. I remember sitting with my mother, stepfather and the doctor when they gave us the prognosis. Patients who go through this treatment have a mortality rate of 3-5 years. Three to five years!

He went through eight chemo and thirty-six radiation treatments. It weakened his immune system causing other complications, but he was able to complete the treatment. The time between his diagnosis and the day he died was approximately three years.

He and my mom only trusted two people to help them during this trying time, me and my step-brother. They relied on me because I lived close, I had a car, and I am compassionate. My mother didn't drive and my stepfather could not drive much of the time. I would take them to radiation treatments. I would go with my mom when he was hospitalized with complications. I would run errands.

This was a very stressful time for all of us. None of us went to a cancer support group. I started smoking again after having quit for five years. My step dad gets lung cancer, and I start smoking again because I'm stressed out. *Does that make any sense!?*

Would the outcome have been different if he had regular medical checkups? Maybe. Maybe he would have known his body better and noticed symptoms sooner. Maybe they could have operated and removed the tumor. Maybe he would have lived an additional two years.

If I had gone to a cancer support group could I have been less stressed and not started smoking again? (I did quit again a few years later). What damage was I doing to myself by smoking?

These experiences with grief and loss, and using drinking and smoking to cope, make me uniquely qualified to help others. I understand the addiction and obsession. I understand losing people and losing yourself. I have recovered, and I am willing to help others to recovery. I can relate my experience to those who have clutter or hoard. I understand being paralyzed by indecision, fear of the unknown, terrified or too proud to ask for help, not wanting to admit that there is something wrong with me.

Well guess what!!! Almost everyone has something wrong with them! And, many die because they don't get help soon enough.

Four

You Can Recover From Clutter

If there is something in our life you do not
want, find the cause and remove it.

— Brian Tracy

My first two years in business I didn't specialize in one particular area. But, I started to notice a pattern in many of my clients. A root cause. One client was disabled and had to leave a job she loved, another retired from a position which defined who she was, one started his own practice after a divorce, another was selling his house after his wife died from a long-term illness, a recent widow had to learn to pay bills and maintain a filing system, and several clients were corporate relocations. A few others had experienced multiple loses in the family within a relatively short period of time. What did they all have in common? Their clutter started to accumulate due to a loss. Loss of a career they loved. Moving out of their comfort zone, away from a community where they were supported, or the home they cherished. Picking up the pieces of their lives after disability, retirement, divorce and the death of a loved one.

And then, in the past year a therapist, whom I had never met, recommended three of her clients to me for professional organizing due to depression and grief.

The clients I worked with one-on-one shared their stories with me while we worked. I sometimes shared my experience with them on grief, alcoholism, addiction to cigarettes, depression or struggles sticking to a diet and exercise program. I shared how I sought help which gave me the strength to go on and succeed. And finally, I tried to instill hope in them that our work together would change them. They were learning new skills, their attitudes and outlook on life would change, they would start to think differently about their stuff.

This is the basis of group therapy, support groups, recovery programs, and peer counseling. Shared experiences help each other. Once you admit that you have a problem you open yourself up to accept help. Once you verbalize a problem it immediately seems a little bit smaller. You can breathe a little easier. Your shoulders start to relax. Sometimes clients cry. That's okay. I offer a hug or a tissue. Peer support is "I have the same problem and here is what I do about it."

That is why we learn most effectively with stories or parables as opposed to lectures, or being told what to do, or being yelled at, or belittled into changing. That's why de-cluttering is not enough. Together we look at the root of the problem. We acknowledge the loss. We see the clutter as just a symptom of the grief, loss, stress, addiction, disability or depression. *I had found my specialty. Due to my personal experience with grief, depression and my recovery from alcoholism, I am uniquely qualified to help others experiencing the same issues. I can reach them when friends, family, therapists, and landlords cannot.*

Once I made this determination, a new flow started to happen which I think you will find amazing. A networking acquaintance and

I started talking. Lisa Purk is a life coach, and the owner of Inner Fire. She helps women with their inner chatter, the self-talk which holds us back. She wanted us to become referral partners. Over time we determined we could use each other's services. She wanted me to reorganize her filing systems. I wanted her to help me implement this new business specialty. So, we traded services. It was a great experience for both of us. She helped me narrow my target market. She encouraged me to change my logo, which I had planned to do since I started my business. She helped me define my goals and take action toward them.

Next, I was asked to speak to a consortium of therapists who meet monthly. The group is called *Women of the North*. Remember the therapist I mentioned earlier? She recommended me for this speaking gig. I finally got to meet her in person that evening when I did my presentation, "Organizing Clients in Grief".

As I prepared for my talk, and to help me understand my new specialty, I had an idea. I would interview a few of my past clients about our work together. These are the questions I asked:

1) What motivated you to ask for help?
2) What contributed to your situation?
3) Describe the feelings that surface when you talk about the clutter.
4) Was there a time when you were organized?
5) Is there a history of clutter or hoarding in the family?
6) Is there addiction, depression, grief, or physical limitations?
7) Have you been or are you currently in therapy or a support group?

These are their stories. Since there is often guilt, shame and embarrassment associated with their clutter, a high level of confidentiality is required between the professional organizer and the client. They have granted me permission to tell you part of their story. Real names and other identifying information has been changed or omitted.

⌒

*D*aisy saw an ad I put in a newspaper. She cut it out and saved it -- *for a year*! Then, she saw me at a talk I was giving. She described me as calm, direct, compassionate, and having insight into what she was trying to overcome. That's when she decided to call me. She had tried help for her disorganization twice in the past. She felt like, "I should know how to do this." And, realized she couldn't.

Several years earlier she was diagnosed with a learning disability. Then, a year later Daisy had stopped working to care for her aging parents. The following year, within a six month period, she lost her mom, dog, aunt and father.

When she talks about her clutter she feels dismay. She describes herself as having a natural inclination to care for others which she puts above all else. This leads to avoidance of her clutter by helping others. She feels an inability to take the first step.

When she sticks with it she can stay organized. But, she has to like doing it. She said, "Mom was the same way as a seamstress. Space was limited in our home, so she put everything away at the end of the day."

She continued, "Mom struggled with organizing, too. Grandma helped. Which is why I may have never learned those skills."

She had a handle on her grief when we met. But, there was some lingering resentment with family members. She was an ex-smoker. And, she had no physical limitations.

At the time that she called me, she was in therapy for depression and attending a support group for her learning disability. She and her therapist agreed she should work with a professional organizer again.

⟶

When I met Rose she said things were a disaster and getting worse. She described me as gentle but persistent. She had a sense that we knew each other already; and, she could be more honest.

Rose lost a parent when she was seven years old. In early adulthood she developed a problem which she sought help for. She was doing well until she lost her parent and step-parent in rapid succession. She stopped following her treatment model for about a year. Then, she got back on track. Then, five years later her husband's parent died.

A year later she asked me for help. She got depressed every time she walked into her house and saw the clutter. She also felt frozen and overwhelmed. She said I made her feel a lot better about herself; and, that I knew just what to do in organizing her stuff which makes maintenance on her part easy.

She doesn't remember ever being organized. She currently has a disability that prevents her from working. But, when she did work she recalls never having the papers she needed for meetings. Her colleagues would carry their papers neatly in a folder. She had never thought to do that.

When asked if there is a history of clutter or hoarding in the family her response was, "Mom had too much stuff to organize."

She does have physical limitations which require physical therapy, and she is treated for depression. She also attends a support group.

⚬

Violet is a young widow with children in elementary school. She had been struggling to keep the house organized in the midst of grieving the sudden death of her husband two years prior to us meeting. She had to take over his role as parent. She needed to keep up with paying the monthly bills which he used to do. She had some help with organizing from a family member. When asked what motivated her to ask me for help she said, "A business colleague of yours suggested you. I don't think I can do this alone, but want it done so I can move forward in a new relationship."

She feels the loss of her husband contributed to the clutter. She wasn't taking enough time to organize and clean. She has a lot of memorabilia from her husband due to his position at work and in the community.

She said the mail just keeps coming. Dealing with it is somewhat of a new skill for her. She feels the benefits of working with a professional organizer have been to go through everything and purge what she no longer needs. Then, find a home for everything.

It's frustrating because she was never this cluttered before. And, there is no history of clutter in the family.

There is no addiction, depression or physical limitation. However, grief is on-going.

Violet and her children were in grief therapy and attending a support group when we worked together.

Five

Understanding Grief

Togetherness

Author Unknown

Death is nothing at all
I have only slipped away into the next room.
Whatever we were to each other,
that we are still.
Call me by my old familiar name,
speak to me in the easy way you always did.
Laugh as we always laughed
at the little jokes we enjoyed together.
Play, smile, think of me, pray for me.
Let my name be the household word it always was.
Let it be spoken without effort.
Life means all that it ever meant.
It is the same as it ever was;
There is absolutely unbroken continuity.

Why should I be out of your mind
because I am out of your sight?
I am but waiting for you, for an interval,
Somewhere very near, just around the corner.
All is well.
Nothing is past; nothing is lost.
One brief moment and all will be as it was before;
only better, infinitely happier, and forever;
We will be together…

Merriam-Webster's definition of grief is:

- deep sadness caused especially by someone's death
- a cause of deep sadness
- trouble or annoyance

One of the earliest memories of my dad was when I was about three years old. He was standing in the hallway of our house, wearing a black suit and he was crying. I had never seen my dad cry before then. He was crying because my grandma died, his mother. She had cancer and they had a hospital bed set up for her in our living room. My mom took care of her.

I had a client who lost an adult daughter. After two years, this is how she describes her grief: "There are days I still want to throw myself on the floor screaming and take a razor blade and cut my skin off. But instead, I accept every offer from friends and family to leave my house and do something."

But what about grief that isn't related to the death of a loved one: parent, grandparent, spouse, child, family pet, etc.? People lose jobs or careers (a part of their identity), homes, connections with their family, romantic break ups, or the use of their body due to disease, disability, or memory impairment.

Here is a mild example. In the 5th grade I started wearing eyeglasses. I had lost something, part of my healthy vision. With corrective lenses the world seemed brighter. But, I got called four-eyes, bookworm, or nerd.

I had also lost one of my passions. My love for swimming and diving diminished. You can't wear your glasses running around the public swimming pool and look cool. And, I had trouble focusing on things clearly without my glasses. But, we all know the saying "kids are resilient, they bounce back quickly". I sought other interests like rollerskating and basketball. However, the emotional scars lasted much longer. There was another saying, "Boys don't make passes at girls who wear glasses". That affected my self-esteem. So, in my sophomore year of high school I started wearing hard contacts. It was a painful process at first. But so worth the pain and aggravation to feel like I fit in more or was more attractive. As time went on contact lenses improved and became more comfortable.

Fast forward to around the age of 40. I loved to read a book while watching TV. Before the invention of the DVR, I would read my murder mysteries during the commercials. I started to notice that my eyes were having trouble making the transition from my book close on my lap to the TV across the room. I saw the eye doctor and he prescribed bifocals. *BIFOCALS!* I was too young for bifocals! But, I liked seeing clearly so I got the bifocals. But I'm cool, so I got the progressive ones without the visible line across the lens, like my grandmother used to wear.

Today, I worry about developing Macular Degeneration, which my mother and her sister have. I know this example is minimal compared to other losses, but it has been a life-time of prescription changes and adjustments with glasses and contact lenses.

When we lose part of ourselves it is like any other loss, to varying degrees. First there is denial. Then there is a grieving process. And, sometimes during the grieving process we get down on ourselves or stuck in depression. We get overwhelmed and sometimes we give up. Some of us struggle though get to the other side which is acceptance. But grief changes us and shapes our attitude and belief system.

I've had a number of losses in my life, before and after recovery: all my grandparents; a 7-year old neighborhood friend of my son's was hit by a car while they were playing together; I've lost four of my five aunts and all of my uncles; several people I knew in recovery who didn't make it; high school friends moved out of state or have passed away; about a dozen family pets; relationship failures.

What's my point? None of them affected me the way my father's death did. Although, the childhood teasing, my self-esteem, my inferiority complex, and a few relationship failures did feed my resentments and contributed to my drinking. However, my out of control downward spiral was triggered by his passing.

People turn to what comforts them or gives them pleasure in their grief. For some, it can be shopping or over eating. For others, it is avoidance behavior. This causes pain, such as getting rid of a loved ones possessions or lack of motivation to clean the house.

Some folks deal with change by writing books on the subject to share their experience. One such book is "When Bad Things Happen to Good People" by Harold S. Kushner.

I had a lot of growing up to do at the age of 35 when, two years after the death of my father, I got sober. So, I read self-help books. This is one of the books I read to help me understand what I had been going through. My grief over my father not only shook my world, it shook my faith in God. In recovery, the basis of which is centered on increasing your spiritual life, I had to find my way back to faith. This book helped.

Rabbi Kushner wrote the book following the death of his son who, at the age of his three, had been diagnosed with progeria or "rapid aging". The doctor described it like this:

"...Aaron would never grow much beyond three feet in height, would have no hair on his head or body, would look like a little old man while he was still a child, and would die in his early teens."

Kushner goes on to say in the introduction of the book on pages 2-5:

"How does one handle news like that? I was a young, inexperienced rabbi, not as familiar with the process of grief as I would later come to be, and what I mostly felt that day was a deep, aching sense of unfairness. It didn't make sense. I had been a good person. I had tried to do what was right in the sight of God. More than that, I was living a more religiously committed life than most people I know, people who had large, healthy families. I believed that I was following God's ways and doing His work. How could this be happening to my family? If god existed, if He was minimally fair, let alone loving and forgiving, how could he do this to me?"

"Every year on Aaron's birthday, my wife and I would celebrate. We would rejoice in his growing up and growing in skill. But we would be gripped by the cold foreknowledge that another year's passing brought us closer to the day when he would be taken from us.

I knew then that one day I would write this book. I would write it out of my own need to put into words some of the most important things I have come to believe and know. And, I would write it to help other people who might one day find themselves in a similar predicament...."

"There were not many books, as there were not many people, to help us when Aaron was living and dying. Friends tried, and were helpful, but how much could they really do? And the books I turned to were more concerned with defending God's honor, with logical proof that bad is really good and that evil is necessary to make this a good world, than they were with curing the bewilderment and the anguish of the parent of a dying child. They had answers to all of their own questions, but no answer for mine.

I hope that this book is not like those....I am fundamentally a religious man who has been hurt by life, and I wanted to write a book that could be given to the person who has been hurt by life – by death, by illness or injury, by rejection or disappointment – and who knows in his heart that if there is justice in the world, he deserved better. What can God mean to such a person? Where can he turn for strength and hope? If you are such a person, if you want to believe in God's goodness and fairness but find it hard because of the things that have happened to you and to people you care about, and if this book helps you do that, then I would have succeeded in distilling some blessing out of Aaron's pain and tears."

"Aaron died two days after his fourteenth birthday."

This chapter is intended to give you a better understanding of the power grief has on some people if not dealt with properly, and how it manifests itself in you or someone you care about. My hope is that you will see the correlation between griefs and clutter the way I do. Please know others see it, too and are willing to help if you want help.

The next chapter goes into more detail on how grieving affects our minds, bodies and pyche.

Six

The Science of Grief

Grief is a universal response to loss, but how
it affects you is a very personal experience.

Depending on what loss we are experiencing, our symptoms may range from sadness, to normal grief or become complicated grief.

Our reactions to having a miscarriage, or losing a family member (including pets), a relative, friend or co-worker may depend on our relationship to that person. Another factor is the manner in which they died, whether the death was after a lengthy battle with cancer, an unexpected death, involved violence, or was a suicide.

The same is true if we grief the loss of a job, house fire, divorce, or end a close relationship or friendship. Our role in the situation also plays an important part in how we grieve. Were we happy in that job or ready to move on to new opportunities? How much was lost in the fire, everything or can we repair the damage? Was the break up one-sided or mutual?

Initially, we may see our reaction solely as an emotional response. Here is an example.

While writing this book my Aunt Dorothy passed away after numerous health issues. She was going through a second round of chemo. She was my dad's sister. I was named after her, she was my godmother, and my confirmation sponsor. Our relationship had its ebbs and flows over our life time, only because life got in the way. Busy, Busy. Busy.

At first, when my cousin called to inform me, I felt sad but I did not cry. I was shocked to hear the news. I had visited her within the least two weeks before she died, and she appeared to be doing fairly well.

When I passed the news onto my mom and sisters, I was sad but I did not cry. Over the next few days memories kept popping to mind. I carried my sadness with me but went through my day to day activities. I was extremely grateful I got to spend some quality time with her. I gathered up pictures to share with relatives at the viewing. I did not cry. I was asked to read from the Bible at her funeral. I got though that without wavering. Then, her daughter sang Ave Marie, and the sound and the song opened a flood gate of tears. And, I cried. And, I felt the permanency of that loss. I still think about her every time I drive past her neighborhood. But, I am no longer sad. I have accepted she is gone.

This is a very sharp contrast to the reaction of losing my father twenty-two years ago. Many factors go into that: my age and experience, the closeness of the relationship, the unexpected death of my father versus the cancer my aunt had treated for years, and my coping skills.

Grief can also affect us physically and psychologically. Studies show that there are physical and neurological aspects of grief.

Here are some common symptoms of grief:

- Shock
- Disbelief
- Sadness
- Guilt

- Anger
- Fear
- Physical symptoms (brought on by stress)

The term grief can be used for other types of losses, such as job loss, divorce, geographic changes and other sources; however, it is important to recognize that the loss resulting from death is irreversible, which cannot be disregarded.

Anticipatory grief: This is the kind of grief experienced when the death of a loved one is just around the corner, such as in cases of terminal illness or an ailing, elderly family member. While painful, some psychologists believe this type of grief may help to shorten the post-death grief process because so many of the related emotions are worked through ahead of time.

Unanticipated grief: This type of grief is often associated with unexpected loss, such as from an accident, heart attack or other surprise event.

Ambiguous grief: This form is the result of a circumstance where there is little or no closure about the unfortunate event. For example, if a loved one is kidnapped and never found, a pet runs away, a parent abandons a child or a child abandons a parent.

There is also *complicated grief* which is listed in the DSM-V as a mental health disorder.

The American Psychological Association (APA) estimates that 15 percent of bereaved people are at risk for developing "complicated grief." According to the APA, this form of grief is more severe than typical grief and is characterized by feelings of meaninglessness, changes in personal beliefs, exaggerated searching or yearning for the deceased, and marked shifts in personal relationships.

Studies on bereavement point to a clear difference between complicated grief and sadness and that complicated grief can activate the neural reward system through the memory of the deceased. In other words, complicated grief and mourning are normal as people feel pain or emotions brought about by the painful memories related to death. However, the areas of reward and addiction were activated in complicated grief.

Grieving individuals are cautioned to avoid alcohol and drugs, because they are depressants and can make the process much more difficult.

According to Mental Health America, a national advocacy group, prolonged grief can trigger anxiety attacks and depression. Other studies show that bereavement has been associated with substance abuse, and research found a greater risk of alcohol-related problems. There is also a high rate of suicide and a 40% rate of depression among the bereaved. Research has found that about a quarter of people who lose their spouse experience clinical depression and anxiety in the first year.

There are also a few studies that used MRI scans to see how the brain changes during grief which correlates to the symptoms we experience. One study reported that the amygdala is involved in sadness because evidence suggests that it plays a role in the anguish of separation.

These are some additional symptoms of complicated grief:

- Continued disbelief in the death of the loved one.
- Being unable to accept the death. Flashback, nightmares, or memories that keep intruding into thoughts over time.

- Severe and prolonged grief symptoms: i.e., anger sadness, or depression.
- Keeping a fantasy relationship with the deceased with the feeling that he or she is always present and watching.
- Continuous yearning and searching for the deceased.
- Unusual symptoms that seem unrelated to the death (physical symptoms, strange or abnormal behaviors).
- Breaking off all social contacts.

Now let's talk about physical symptoms. Stress, anxiety, depression and grief all have the potential to impact our health by suppressing our immune system. In an article written by Dr. Sanjay Gupta titled *How Grief Can Make You Sick*, she states, "Losing a loved one is an emotionally painful experience that can have a real effect on the mind and body. She goes on to quote M. Katherine Shear, MD, professor of psychiatry at Columbia University and director of the Center for Complicated Grief; "The best way to understand how grief can affect your health is to understand what bereavement entails: one, a major stressor; and two, loss of a close relationship."

Grief makes us susceptible to diseases such as the common cold, sore throats and other infections. Other diseases shown to be connected to the stress of grief are ulcerative colitis, rheumatoid arthritis, asthma, heart disease and cancer. The connection between the mind and body is not always recognized, but there is real scientific evidence that what we think and feel has a direct effect on our biological systems. In her book *Surviving Grief . . . and Learning to Live Again*, psychologist Catherine M. Sanders, PhD, writes that the bereaved can "become so weak that we actually feel like we have the flu… this weakness frightens and perplexes us."

Among the most common physical responses to loss are changes in our sleep patterns and low energy. Sleeping normally after a loss would be unusual. At a subconscious level, you may not want to lose any more control by sleeping. Therefore, you may have difficulty getting to sleep; or, waking early and having trouble getting back to sleep. During grief your body needs more rest than usual.

This ties into low energy, exhaustion, and fatigue which are also normal responses. You may also find yourself getting tired more quickly, sometimes even at the start of the day. You may have difficulty thinking clearly.

These are all ways your body may react to losses that you encounter in life.

- Muscle aches and pains
- Shortness of breath
- Feelings of emptiness in your stomach
- Tightness in your throat or chest
- Digestive problems
- Sensitivity to noise
- Heart palpitations
- Queasiness or nausea
- Headaches
- Increased allergy symptoms
- Changes in appetite, leading to weight loss or gain
- Agitation/tension

Dr. Gupta goes on to say, "The emotional impact of grief is often described as "heartache" or "heartbreak," but the release of stress hormones associated with grief can cause actual cardiac problems."

Dr. Shear explains: "We know a fair amount about how stress affects the cardiovascular and immune systems, namely by activating both, and in vulnerable people this leads to increased rates of cardiovascular disease and cancer. Acute stress can also cause something called stress cardiomyopathy which is an acute form of cardiac illness."

One study found that the incidence of an acute heart attack increases 21-fold within 24 hours of the death of a loved one, before declining steadily with each subsequent day. In another study, British researchers found that older people who are grieving are more likely to have weakened immune systems and develop infections.

According to the British Psychological Society, there is the commonly known "broken heart syndrome", also termed stress or takotsubo cardiomyopathy. It usually follows "significant emotional or physical stress", according to the British Heart Foundation. The heart muscle suddenly becomes weakened and one of the heart's chambers changes shape. It's thought that it affects 100 people per million each year.

This is why it is paramount that we take care of our physical needs during this vulnerable time. Another reason self-care is vitally important is if we have others we are still responsible for such as children or aging parents. We must take care of ourselves first in order to be there to help care for them.

And, this is where our "WE" can help us in the process, by ensuring we don't give up on self-care, or giving us respite from caring for others.

Ruth Sisson states in her book, *Moving Beyond Grief...Lessons From Those Who Have Lived Through Sorrow:*

"Having loving, caring people in your life is essential to recovery from grief....Friends who give us the gift of their time and attention can speed the emotional healing process, and can even help us avoid the physical illness that often come from keeping toxic emotions stuffed down inside us...we need patient, available people who will say, "I'm here for you, at any time, for any reason.""

Seven

Healthy Ways of Addressing Grief

*Something very beautiful happens to people
when their world has fallen apart: a humility,
a nobility, a higher intelligence emerges at just
the point when our knees hit the floor.*

— Marianne Williamson

About two and a half years after my father's death, after ending my marriage and trying to stay sober, I attended grief counseling through my church. The same church I received all the Catholic sacraments in: baptism, communion, confirmation, marriage. The same church through which my dad was buried. The church I turned my back on in the last two years of my drinking.

There were nine people there trying to cope with their losses. One was a young mother whose one day old son had not survived. I had recently received a one month sobriety coin. I gave her that coin and explained to her that WE take life one day at a time. I told her she should have it and I hoped that it would bring her some comfort.

I did this because I felt the pain of her loss too. And, I felt that her loss was a greater than my own. I had 33 years with my loved one. She had nine months and one day. I have memories, good and bad, with my dad. She did not.

It put into perspective for me that everyone's loss is different. People in our grief counseling group lost a father, husband, son, mother, friend, or sister. Our loved one ranged in age from 1-day old to 70 years old.

It also helped close an old wound left open between me and my ex-husband. He and my father did not get along. My husband went out of town to work during my dad's funeral. I held a resentment about his absence in my time of need. And, I was drunk or hung over through most of the original funeral. In trying to stay sober I was learning that my unresolved resentments and anger were potential triggers to lead me back to drinking.

At the end of grief counseling, the facilitator held a memorial service. This helped me properly say good-bye. I invited my ex-husband and explained to him what I was trying to do with my sobriety and grief. He agreed to attend. My communication with him and his act of kindness helped me heal a little more through that process. I saved much of the printed information I received at grief counseling to this day. However, I would like to reprint something I received more recently.

Stephanie Roy is a Process Counselor whom I met through the Women's Business Network (WBN) early in my new career. She is also trained in 12th Step work. Every month our National Association of Professional Organizers (NAPO) Pittsburgh chapter has a speaker the second hour after our business meeting. This helps us with continuing education credits (CEU). I suggested Stephanie speak to our group about understanding grief and loss. In her presentation she distributed the "20 Tips for Good Grieving", a handout reprinted from the website the Good Grief Center for Bereavement Support (GGC), www.goodgriefcenter.com. I've kept that handout ever since that day because I believe it to be "spot on" to my experience with grief.

20 tips for good grieving

1. Talk about your loss with friends, family or a professional. Grief is a process, not an event.
2. Grief is work, requiring time and energy. The memories, meanings and fulfilled needs provided by the lost loved one take time to work through.
3. Let yourself enter the emotions of grief. Grievers tend naturally to avoid the painful emotions. Losing someone close to you means you deserve to allow yourself to feel all your emotions – sadness, anger, intense longing, guilt and others.
4. Consider writing your loved one a letter. Say what you would tell them as if it were your last chance. Even if you never share the letter with anyone, writing it may help you work through your grief.
5. Resume your life but leave time and space for grieving. Life marches on for the living. But try to resist the temptation to "throw yourself" into work or other diversions. This leaves too little time for the grief work you need to do for yourself.
6. Take care of yourself. You have been wounded. Something very valuable and dear has been taken away from you. Give yourself time and space to begin healing. Get enough rest. Eat nourishing food. Give yourself a break.
7. Resist the temptation to use alcohol or drugs to numb your pain. These can interfere with the grieving process by delaying it or covering it up.

8. If you have any religious inclination, consider contacting your place of worship. All religions recognize that grievers need special help. Consider taking advantage of these services even if you have not been attending regularly. You will not be turned away.

9. Consider seeking out other grievers. Someone who has also been through grief can empathize with you, and vice versa. Organizations like The Compassionate Friends or THEOS* recognize the value of sharing in a group setting.

10. Don't feel obligated to join groups if they are not for you. The grief process is highly individual. Some people prefer solitude or reflection rather than group work. Do what feels right for you.

11. Don't neglect your own health. Grieving puts a heavy burden of stress on your body. It can disturb sleep patterns, lead to depression, weaken your immune system, and worsen medical problems that had been stable, such as high blood pressure. Take prescribed medications and get regular check-ups. If you suffer from disabling insomnia or anxiety, see your doctor. Sometimes short-term medication can be very helpful.

12. Get help for severe or persistent depression. Someone once said: "grief is not a disease but it can become one." Grief can lead to serious depression. Consider getting professional help if you feel overwhelmed, hopeless, or helpless. Other signs of depression can include sleep impairment (too little or too much), appetite or weight change, low energy, difficulty concentrating, and feeling listless or agitated. By all means, seek professional help if you have suicidal thoughts.

13. Grief work can become complicated. Mixed emotions (positive and negative feelings), unresolved emotional turmoil and losing someone after an argument can complicate the grieving

process. Sharing these feelings with a professional therapist can help. Grief therapy need not be a long-term commitment. Even if you don't see yourself as the kind of person who seeks therapy, this may be beneficial.

14. Anger is common in normal grieving and certainly justified when a loved one dies due to the malevolence of others. Try venting your anger in a letter. Consider channeling your anger into constructive action. Volunteer to work for causes that seek justice and prevention. Spending your energy helping someone else can help you in the process.

15. Allow time to grieve. One to two years is not a long time to allow yourself to work through grief. We need to remind ourselves that the healing process cannot be rushed; it will proceed at its own rate.

16. Be patient. The grieving process often includes setbacks. Don't expect to set an "I'll be over it" deadline and succeed. Often, grieving resumes after a time, sometimes even months or years. Reminders can trigger a flood of emotions. Don't be surprised if this happens, and don't consider it a sign of weakness. Instead, your psyche is telling you more grief work needs to be done.

17. At some point those who have lost a partner or love companion will face the decision of whether to be open to a new relationship. Consider imagining the situation reversed. That is, if you died and your lover or spouse survived, what would you want them to do? It may help you to see your situation from this angle.

18. If you feel stuck in your grief, try a new approach. We are creatures of habit who learn very quickly how to avoid painful situations. However, this may hinder working through the entirety of your grief. To "jump start" the process, consider

reviewing memorabilia, photos, home movies, or videos. Talk about your loved one at holidays when his or her absence is most obvious. Don't avoid it so as not to spoil the festivities. This is the perfect time to check in with other family members about how they're doing with grief work, and share mutual support.

19. Create your own memorial service. Celebrate their lifetime accomplishments, values, and principles. Consider carrying the torch of a cause they believed in as a memorial. Start a scholarship, plant a garden, or make a donation in their name.

20. The grieving process has run its course when you feel weary of rehashing events and memories and finally accept the fact the your loved one can remain with you only in spirit. For some, the process never really ends; it just gets easier over time. You will know you are ready to move forward when you feel you can reinvest the energy once invested in your loved one in a new place. This takes time. Good grief means being good to yourself during the process.

__International Theos Foundation:__ An international support network for recently widowed men and women; to sponsor programs and provide services to help participants work through their immediate grief and cope with day-to-day practical concerns of widowhood.

Professional organizers deal with clients who are in some stage of transition in life: raising a family, separation or divorce, starting a business, loss of a business, retirement, death of a loved one, a medical disability, downsizing from the family home into assisted living, and the list goes on.

Now here is another definition of grief taken from the Institute of Challenging Disorganization (ICD) Publication No. 018 "Helping the Grieving Client".

"Grief is an individual's reaction to, and the process of dealing with, change and loss.

Change is difficult for living things, including human beings. Biologically, we are genetically programmed, "hard-wired" if you will, for stability, or homeostasis in scientific terms. When the world is stable around us (and that includes the stability of our bodies and minds, we are in control: when there is change, there is initial chaos and we lose control. That means it is difficult for us to have to deal with change; it produces stress. Usually, sooner or later depending on a whole host of factors, we create something new out of that chaos. We are permanently changed. "

"Grief, then…is the process one goes through to deal with the change and loss, and eventually to become able to build something new out of the experience. It is normal, and necessary to go through this process whenever there is change. The change can be so small that we are unaware of it, or it can be profound and overwhelming."

This is why a slow steady buildup of clutter can go unnoticed or not be a priority for someone who is in transition. Then, it becomes too overwhelming to deal with so it grows more. Then it becomes a part of the norm. Some people become oblivious to it, they go into denial, become defensive, and are too ashamed to ask for help.

If we can address the underlying root cause of their grief or trauma at the same time that we address the mess, I believe they have a better chance of success in maintaining their organized space. Professional organizers understand that getting therapy for chronic disorganization which stems from various factors is a vital part of the team approach. They will begin to live a whole life once again.

The Weaver
Author unknown

The pattern of my life has changed,
For life has brought a sorrow;
The pattern must be rearranged
To fit a new tomorrow.

Although my eyes are blind with tears,
Although my heart is weary,
Tomorrow's duties still appear
Even though today is dreary.

The pattern of my life is mine,
A thing that must be finished
Though time has altered its' design,
Its' brightness has diminished.

A little kneeling by my bed,
Some hours of quiet grieving
And then I must take up my thread of life
And carry on the weaving.

Eight

ORGANIZING PRINCIPLES

People change for two main reasons: Their minds have been opened, or their hearts have been broken.

— SPIRIT SCIENCE

The old saying goes, "Don't look a gift horse in the mouth". But as I embarked on this new career, and read book after book on organizing, I discovered I really had a natural gift. I like to call it my super power. It made me wonder why I can keep myself organized when other people lack this skill. What do I habitually do that others find a struggle?

I know some of it was instilled in me and my sisters by my parents. We lived in an organized home. There were only two areas of the house I remember being cluttered: the steps going to the second floor and the landing going at the top of the stairs to the basement.

There were five of us living in a two bedroom house. One of my sisters and I always shared the third floor attic as a bedroom. So for convenience, we left our shoes on both sides of the steps which went to the second floor. There was a small stairwell just off of the dining room at the top of the basement stairs. We used this area to hang all of our coats.

My father was adamant that everything had to be in its place or have a home. If you wanted to stay on his good side, you would put things back where they belonged, and you would return things that you borrowed. We were also responsible to clean up after ourselves and to clean our rooms.

We were also taught by nuns in the catholic school system. If you did not "toe the line" they were allowed to hit, punish or humiliate you in some fashion. More incentive to be organized. The definition of "toe the line" is: *To do what you are ordered or expected to do. Meet a standard, abide by the rules.*

So, perhaps naturally, one of the first articles I wrote after becoming a professional organizer was entitled, "Secrets of the Super Organized". And, one of the first presentations I created was "Organizing 101". I also typed up a tip sheet to hand out.

I have reprinted them on the following page so you can reference them easily, or copy them out of the book and post them wherever you will see them every day to motivate you and remind you.

There is nothing mysterious about being organized. They are not really secrets as much as they are habits anyone can put into practice. Please try and remember that you are learning a new skill like swimming, riding a bike, telling time, driving a stick shift, speaking a foreign language, or playing an instrument. IT TAKES PRACTICE!

These tips were developed based on one of the first organization books I read. The author of *Organizing from the Inside Out*, Julie Morganstern, created the acronym SPACE:

Sort   *assign a home* ⟶ *ongoing*
Purge   *containerize*   *maintenance*

Dorothy L. Clear, CPO

Sort
Purge
Assign a <u>home</u>
Containerize
Equalize [ongoing <u>maintenance</u>]

"The key to succeeding with the SPACE formula is to do *every one* of the steps, and, most important, do them *in order*."

Organizing 101 Tip Sheet

1. Schedule time with yourself to do the project.
2. Choose one area to organize and stay focused on that one area: shelf, counter, closet, drawer, medicine cabinet.
3. Sort through all the items in the space you are organizing.
4. Purge items you no longer need: broken, stained, almost empty, never opened or used, doesn't fit.
   NOTE: Having a patient, understanding, compassionate friend or family member can be vital to helping you in this step.
5. Organize all like items together in one spot.
   Bathroom – dental care, hair care, hair accessories, lotions, feminine products.
   Bedroom - **closet**: skirts, dresses, pants, robes, suits, blouses, purses, hats.
6. Assign every category a home in that space.
7. Containerize – make sure you have the right size container for that category; i.e. small items in small containers, medium items in medium containers, etc. Shop for decorative containers that suit your décor or style.
8. Label (optional) – make handmade labels, or buy sticky labels or tags with ribbons. Use your creativity and imagination.

Develop Good Habits ⭐

Do it now. When I think of something that needs done, I do it right away, if possible, before I forget. Or, I write it on a to-do list. Perhaps it is 12 noon and I remember I am supposed to water the outside flowers today. But it is too hot at noon. So, I write it on my to-do list for 7pm. If I remember that I have clothes in the dryer, I go get them and fold them. I put the laundry basket next to the stairs so I remember to take it up stairs the next time I go to the second floor bedroom.

Create visual cues. For grocery shopping I keep reusable bags in the trunk of my car. After I unpack the food, I fold the bags and put them next to my purse. So, the next time I leave the house, the bags go back in the trunk of the car.

Get into routines. At night when I undress, my clothes go in one of two places. If the garment is not soiled, it goes back in the drawer or closet to be worn one more time before it gets washed. Or, it goes in the laundry basket to be washed. My shoes also go in the closet every night. My jewelry gets put in my jewelry box. I make my bed each morning because I love the way it pulls the room together.

Everything has a place. Designating a home for everything enables me to find it when I need it. I always put items back where they belong after I use them. Sometimes I have multiples around the house for convenience. I have nail clippers in the end table drawer in the living room, in my purse, in the bathroom medicine cabinet, and in the drawer of my side table next to my bed.

Pick up after yourself. If I am covered up with a blanket while watching TV in the living room, I fold it and put it in our storage chest when I am done. When I leave the living room, I take my empty drinking glass to the kitchen. It either gets placed on the sink counter to be reused or in the dishwasher.

Make it easy to get started. Keep tools & supplies where you use them. I have cleaning products in the kitchen, basement laundry room, and under the sink in the second floor bathroom. I keep scissors in my bedroom, craft room, living room end table, kitchen drawer and home office.

Solve the daily frustrations. Buy products or repurpose furniture that help you remain sane. I couldn't stand my pot lids laying stacked on top of each other in the bottom of the cabinet. At the local hardware store I found a rack that holds lids. Inside the dining room sideboard was a disorganized catch-all until I bought two folding stand up shelves to reorganize the clutter. Pet supplies litter our pantry counter. The simple solution was to put it all in a plastic bin.

Assign drop spots for each family member. There is limited counter space in our kitchen. My husband would come home from work and put his stuff all over the countertop. I moved a small 12" x 12" table we had and placed it near the front door for him to use. I also bought a key holder and attached it to the wall above the table for all of us. My step-daughter has a spot near the back door where there is a small bench and hooks for her jackets and scarves. My space is a three-tiered shelf unit next to the dining room sideboard.

I hope you find these tips easy to understand. It's a bit harder to put them into practice, but make a start and refer back to this list often. You will be in the habit of staying organized in no time at all. It will amaze you, your friends and family, by just how much time and money you will save in the future. The stress, anxiety, fear, depression, tension will lessen. You will be able to spend time enjoying the company of others.

Motivation Tips

Now, how do you get and keep yourself motivated? When I thought about writing this book, I was doing some research and came across a Declaration of Author Intention. I printed it out, signed it and hung it on the wall. Next I found an editor. Well, actually we found each other. She was one of my clients. Coincidence???

After four chapters, the book stalled. Then, I got an accountability partner. She holds me accountable to plan when I am going to write each week and follow through. We email and text each other to ensure I am keeping my commitment. She has tasks for herself each week, also. We talk on the phone every other week to establish new tasks and goals.

When I want to set goals and objectives for my business, I write them down. I tie in rewards for myself with weekly goals I achieve. I also reward myself and my family members for new achievements that I reach. This helps them support my efforts.

In starting any type of new company, group or club, it's advisable to write out a vision and a mission statement.

When I begin working with a new client I ask them what are their priorities, visions, and goals for the space we are organizing.

This is the WHY of what you are doing. What is your WHY?

Here are some samples of what your WHY might look like:

- I can't do it all. I need to be a good role model for my children. They need to learn these skills from me.
- All this clutter is causing real conflict with my spouse. I'm afraid he or she will divorce me. I'm tired of arguing about it. I want to stay together and have a happy marriage.
- I want to be able to invite my children and grandchildren to visit me for holidays and birthdays.

- I want to feel relaxed and productive in my home office. This back-log of filing drives me crazy. I need a system to keep up with it.
- It would be nice to entertain friends but I'm too ashamed of all this clutter.
- I want my garage or spare room to function for its intended purpose.

You may use this space (NOW) to set your intention, list your "why", or set your goals and objectives. Write out what you want to achieve. If you have a deadline, state that as well. Keep these things in mind:

- My intention is an important step.
- It is the first of several steps I will take.
- My goals and my own growth happen together.
  Donna Kosik, Author Starter Kit.

_____

_____

_____

_____

_____

_____

_____

_____

Nine

Getting Additional Help

Fix your eyes forward on what you can do,
not back on what you cannot change.

– Tom Clancy

If you have given this, and I mean REALLY given this a good solid try for several weeks, and show little progress you may be churning. That means moving things from one place to another without sorting and purging. Remember the final step is organizing what you really love and need.

If you have tried different methods of getting organized and have given up trying to do it alone, it is time for outside help. Remember there is no shame in asking for help. We all need a little help sometime. I believe those that succeed have the willingness to admit when they cannot do something on their own and ask for guidance.

We had a speaker at one of our monthly NAPO Pittsburgh meetings that said something that really stuck with me. He was there to share his story with us on how challenging it was to live with ADHD

(Attention Deficit Hyperactivity Disorder). As an adult he accepted himself, learned about his condition, and got appropriate treatment. That enabled him to function. But what enabled him to succeed was that he worked on his strengths and built up a team of people in his company that could support his weakness. They did the things he struggled with while he was free to do the things at which he excelled.

So after reading this book, at the very least, I hope you are motivated to look at your strengths and weaknesses, ask for help and start building your team.

When I am at a crossroads, cannot make a decision, or need motivation, I turn to the 3 C's - - Counseling, Confidant, or Cleric.

- Counseling: emotion, venting, problem-solving
- Confidant: help in a specific area (painter, plumber, professional organizer, accountant, business mentor, sales trainer, teacher)
- Cleric: spiritual motivator, cheerleader, deep thinker

Most likely you have heard or seen the words "Mind, Body, Spirit" together in the context of wholeness or wellbeing. Many will have preconceived notions of therapy, a certain level of pride or stubbornness in asking for help, and, very different views on religion vs. spirituality. But what it really boils down to is someone to talk to who may be able to provide you with new insight or perspective. You've no doubt heard someone say things like:

- "I'd never talk to a shrink."
- "I don't need to talk to anyone. I can handle this."
- "Leave me alone about it"
- "I can get over this."
- "It's just a phase; it'll pass."
- "Snap out of it."

- "I hate church."
- "I don't practice religion."
- "If there is a God, why does he let bad things happen to good people?"
- "I used to pray, but nothing happened, so I quit"

First of all, seeking counsel doesn't mean you are weak and it doesn't have to mean psychotherapy, brainwashing or being institutionalized. It can empower you to live the life you imagine for yourself.

Counseling. This can look very different depending on the circumstances you are facing. The times I sought counseling in my life range from facing issues of abandonment to the inability to handle my emotions to dealing with grief to recovery from alcoholism. Those times were spent talking to the school counselor, a Catholic Charities nun/therapist, participation in a grief support group, and attending a hospital outpatient rehab. Those challenging times in my life stunted my personal growth, but by talking to a licensed professional and getting all that self-chatter out of my head set me back on the right path. Maybe you don't know why you are struggling. Seek help anyway. A mental health professional will complete an assessment and refer you to the appropriate person or group. The main thing is to be HONEST with them and yourself!!!

Resources can be found by referral from a friend or your doctor, an internet search in your area, or your county health department. If you have sound insight into what is troubling you seek out a specialist in that area.

Do I have prejudices about counseling?

_____

_____

_____

I will call _____ to find out more information.

What I hope to accomplish by completing this step is:

_____

_____

_____

NOTE: Not everyone with clutter needs counseling. But you may benefit if the root cause has to do with your mental health such as grief, depression, anxiety, substance abuse, dementia, ADHD, ADD, trauma, a brain injury, OCD, etc.

Confidant. What do you think of when you hear the word confidant? What comes to my mind is the theme song from the NBC sitcom <u>The Golden Girls</u>.

Thank you for being a friend
Traveled down the road and back again
Your heart is true, you're a pal and a confidant.
Lyrics by Andrew Gold, 1978

The definition is "a person with whom one shares a problem, a secret, or a private matter, trusting them not to repeat it to others."

In other words, this does not mean gossip about others. It is about what is affecting you from moving forward. It is the action of confiding in another person to get to a resolution. There is an old idiom that states, "A problem shared is a problem halved". By opening up to another person, we are freeing ourselves from a heavy burden. A variation on that is "Shared grief is half grief".

Choose this person carefully. Trust is of utmost importance. If trust is broken it is very hard to fix and could make the problem worse.

Ever since my business was in the conception stage, I have relied on the advice of others. I asked friends how much they would pay for my services. I tried out different business names with a business colleague. I did informational interviews with people in the same field. I asked an accountant if I was doing my financial spreadsheet appropriately. I worked with a sales coach to set goals and a life coach to help me implement them.

My big sister, Stephanie Scanlon, purchased a franchise of Decorating Den Interiors several months before I started my company. Our livelihoods complement each other; design and organizing. I watched what she did and asked her questions. She introduced me to networking and marketing groups. We actually worked for each other on occasion early in our businesses. We collaborated on speaking engagements. We are referral partners. She is one of my confidants.

List some people you could use as a confidant:

_____   _____

_____   _____

_____   _____

Cleric. For lack of a better word, someone who will advise you in spiritual matters. Examples: priest, reverend, pastor, sky pilot, Holy Joe, chaplain, confessor, deacon, vicar, sponsor, path finder.

Spiritual – related to the spirit or soul, not of physical nature or matter, intangible.

There are seven Catholic sacraments. I have received five of them. My parents had me Baptized when I was an infant. They sent me to Catholic grade school and high school where I also received the Eucharist, Reconciliation, and Confirmation. As an adult I received the sacrament of Holy Matrimony when I married my first husband. The other two are Holy Orders (ordination) and Anointing of the Sick (last rites).

I stopped practicing my Catholicism sometime between my father dying, my divorce and getting sober. Occasionally, I would try it again. It was a part of me. It was ingrained in my belief system. Maybe I'd go to church around the major holy days like Lent, Easter, Advent and Christmas. I have tried different Catholic churches. I have attended Christian, Methodist, Baptist and Presbyterian services. But, there are many things I don't agree with in organized religion. I don't fit in. I have accepted that. Other people may not and that's okay.

Once I understood my authentic self, I started practicing spirituality in the form of prayer and meditation. But mostly prayer. I have a spiritual advisor to keep my self-will, ego and pride in check. She is who I turn to when I am angry, resentful, when I think I have made a mistake and need to make an apology. Or, when I have a gigantic decision to make.

My life is filled with gratitude, balance, and principles to live by. I continually work on developing my character. I try to stay out of other people's business.

My life is wonderful!!!

Many people turn their back on God when something tragic happens to them. I disagree with this theory. I believe humankind has self-will. When self-will is not in line with God (*The Great Spirit, your Higher Power, the positive energy of the universal, Mother Nature*), that is when and why bad things happen. All my strength comes from prayer to what I believe in. So, define what you believe in and make a start. Seek guidance from another but put your trust in one of the above.

This takes practice if you are starting from scratch. Keep practicing. You are worth it. The results with be amazing. You will see everyday miracles you used to ignore. You will feel joy. Start the journey today.

How will you define the entity you believe in?

_____
_____
_____

Whom can you talk to that will help you with your spirituality and faith:

_____
_____

Ten

Embracing a New Way of Living

*And the day came when the risk to remain tight in a
bud was more painful than the risk it took to blossom.*

— Anais Nin

If you have read this far in the book… ***Congratulations*!!!**

Toot your horn!   **Dance a jig!**   **Shout hooray!**

Many people have organizing books but never finish reading them or implementing the program as it is laid out. Nor do they use the book as a resource to turn back to again and again until it becomes a new way of living. That is basically how I built my library early on in my career. My organizing clients would have book lying around and say, "You take the book and read it. Then, tell me how to do it." "You take it; it hasn't done me any good." "I never read it." So again I say CONGRATULATIONS!!!

The next step is to choose a planner or calendar, just one, and use it **exclusively.** No more small pieces of paper, or stickie notes everywhere. If you must write a note transfer it to your planner. Or, keep ONE notebook with your calendar and write all your notes in that ONE notebook. Keep all your addresses and contact information in ONE place: an address book, a phone app, a spreadsheet. First, I revived my old Franklin Covey Planner. This planner had served me well in my previous corporate life. Then the smart phone hit the market, a hand-held computer that could do everything my planner did and takes up less space. I switched and have never looked back. Then, there is one spiral note pad on my desk for phone messages and daily to-do-lists. For tasks which need to be completed for other organizations I belong to and activities that need to be planned out, I use an index card system on my white board.

This next step is where I struggled. Writing down goals. Off and on during my life I have set goals for specific dreams or accomplishments. Sometimes I wrote them down and sometimes I did not. I would try to keep it all in my head. For example, if I needed to read a novel for a college course I would divide the total number of pages by the time frame to complete it to determine how many pages per day I needed to read. I probably did not write that one down and track whether or not I was meeting my goal.

Another example would be when I decided to take my trip of a lifetime to Italy. This involved numerous steps which included: applying for a loan through my credit union, signing up for the guided tour, getting a passport, researching the weather at that time of year so I would know what to pack, brushing up on my language skills, etc. For this adventure, I wrote out a to-do list and made a check list of what to pack.

But writing down goals as an on-going part of my life eluded me, and made me feel inadequate whenever the topic was brought up in conversation. I made half-hearted attempts, tried different methods, and finally gave up and avoided doing it altogether.

However, in order to succeed in running my own business I could not and should not avoid it any longer.

So, being the Do-It-Yourselfer that I am, I have found a few methods that work for me. More importantly though, I was taught by my business coach, Dan Hudock (Sandler Training), the method that I use most consistently and successfully.

Here are some suggestions to try, along with a sample of what Dan taught me. If you try one consistently for a few weeks and then quit, it's okay. Like falling off your diet, just get started again. If you find one doesn't work for you or you just cannot stick to it, then try another one. If none of them fit you, find a method that does, or seek outside help. Do not get impatient, talk down to yourself or give up. (Review the Philosophies in the appendix.)

Method One: <u>Write down three goals each day.</u>
It's okay if you don't get them done and it's okay if you get more done. But start with three. Three goals per day is realistic. If you complete your daily goals 85-90% of the time…image how much you will accomplish! Now image how many you accomplish if you don't follow this advice. Some is better than none. Progress not perfection.

NOTE: A caution about perfectionist. It can become a form of procrastination. In the book titled, "Buried in Treasures" by Randy Frost, David Tolin and Gail Steketee, they wrote:

"...when most of us think of a "perfectionist," we think of someone whose home is immaculately clean, with everything in its place, and so on. But for some people, perfectionism works in a slightly different way. They become so afraid of making the wrong decision that the prospect of making decisions gives rise to strong feelings of anxiety and worry. As a result, the person tends to avoid the decision-making process altogether. The basic operating principle seems to be, "If I can't be sure of doing it exactly right, I'd better not do it at all." Paradoxically, therefore, the person's perfectionist beliefs contribute to his or her home becoming the model of imperfection."

When you write down your goals, make them SMART. According to Smart-Goals-Guide.com:

*When the S.M.A.R.T goal was first introduced to the world it was an acronym which stood for **S**pecific, **M**easureable, **A**ssignable, **R**ealistic, **T**ime-based.*

The SMART acronym first appeared in the November 1981 issue of Management Review. "There's a S.M.A.R.T. way to write management goals and objectives." was the title and it was written by George Doran, Arthur Miller, and James Cunningham. Initially it was seen as a business tool and thousands of people across the world were taught how to use it. This was often used as part of improving project management processes in business.

When it came to creating project objectives, George Doran's framework was the way used to define and agree consensus on goals - it still is.

Today smart goals are used by people right across the world, for setting all sorts of goals; work and career goals, health goals, financial goals, personal development goals to name a few...."

Many variations have developed over time. My suggestion is to keep it simple by using **Specific, Measureable, Attainable, Relevant, and Time-based**. But, feel free to research this and change it to apply to your world.

Method Two: <u>Compile a To-Do List</u>
Instead of keeping all the things I want to accomplish in my head, I write a longer to-do list. This I use to draw my three goals for each day. It also allows me to break larger tasks down into smaller, more manageable tasks.

Method Three: <u>Weekly Goals</u>
This method and the next I learned from my Sandler coach. I have a list for personal goals and a separate list with business goals. List up to seven goals to accomplish each week. The number in parenthesis is the number of days in a week you wish to complete the task. Circle the days as each goal is completed. If 90% of the goals are completed, there is a reward earned. If you do not meet the 90%, NO REWARD. This method allows you to track you goals.

Example of personal goals:

Meet or talk to one friend (1)	S	S	M	T	W	Th	F
Walk 30 min. (3)	S	S	M	T	W	Th	F
Whiten teeth (1)	S	S	M	T	W	Th	F
Train puppy ½ hour (2)	S	S	M	T	W	Th	F
Organizing 15 min before bed (5)	S	S	M	T	W	Th	F

TOTAL 12 (90%=10)
Reward for doing 10 out of 12 – Take-out food Friday night.

Example of business goals:

Post to social media (5)	S	S	M	T	W	Th	F
Write for 2 hours (1)	S	S	M	T	W	Th	F
Hold 1:1 meeting (1)	S	S	M	T	W	Th	F
Make 3 sales calls (3)	S	S	M	T	W	Th	F
Update financial data (1)	S	S	M	T	W	Th	F
Talk to accountability partner (1)	S	S	M	T	W	Th	F
Prospect for presentations (1)	S	S	M	T	W	Th	F
Read industry information 1 hour (3)	S	S	M	T	W	Th	F

Total 16 (90%=14)
Reward – Reload $15 on Starbucks gold card

Method Four: Level Up-Earn Reward

This is another spin on the above goals and rewards chart with Big Picture thinking. Say you are ready to tackle organizing your entire home. This is what your chart may look like.

Goals & Rewards Chart for Organizing Your Home

	REWARD	REWARD	REWARD
ACCOMPLISHMENT	Me	Spouse	Children
Garage			
Pantry			
Spare bedroom			
Child's room – closet			
Child's room - drawers			
Dining room – table			
Dining room - buffet			
Kitchen – top cabinets			
Kitchen – bottom cabinets			
Refrigerator			
Laundry room			
Livingroom			
Basement Shelves			
Basement Corner			

Each family member writes a list of small rewards such as new fishing lure, facial, pizza Saturday night, movie tickets, lunch out, new baseball glove, massage, manicure, new dress for doll, Latte, concert tickets, team jersey, new fish, etc. Use those lists to fill in the blanks in each person's column. For each goal that is completed the whole family is rewarded!!! This helps the family support your goals and helps you achieve them. Draw a line through the area you have completed and the goals that were earned.

Method Five: <u>Task Board</u>

If you are involved in several committees, organizations, or need to keep track of all the kid's activities, you may benefit from using a task board. Here is how I use mine. Write the master categories on the top card. Below each master category are the tasks or activities cards associated with each heading. Draw a line through the tasks you finish.

NAPO Pittsburgh	Marketing/ Presentations	Hoarding Task Force	Networking Group
Bylaws	Publicize talk	~~Draft donate letter~~	Invite colleague
Retreat	Prep for class	Sub-committee mtg.	~~Topic suggestion~~
Ethics class	~~Update website~~		

Your board might look like this:

Book Club	Girl Scouts	Band Booster	Choir
~~Read chapter 3~~	Next activity	Update member list	~~Suggest music~~
Host June's mtg.	Order badges	Suggest Fundraiser	Schedule practice
Pick next book		~~Create form~~	

The final step is maintenance. Practice your new system consistently and build routines into your day.

- Plan your day first thing in the morning or the night before.
- Keep a running grocery list, inventory what you have before you shop.
- Plan you weekly meals as there are numerous benefits.
- Sort through your mail daily near a trash can or recycling bin.
- Do a 10-minute clean sweep of your bedroom before bedtime.
- Make picking up toys fun with your kids or a competition.
- Return items to their permanent home.
- Fill one grocery bag to throw away each day.
- Be accountable to someone, especially if you live alone.
- Get the whole family involved. This may take constant gentle reminders or family meetings.
- Sort through clothes when the seasons change.
- Have an established donation box or bag at the ready for when you decide you no longer want an item.
- File away your most important papers and vital records in one safe place.
- Update your goals.

These are meant to be suggestions only. You will need to compile your own list of maintenance steps to suit your lifestyle.

Eleven

PASS IT ON

When an old farmer's stallion wins a prize at a country show, his neighbour calls round to congratulate him, but the old farmer says, "Who knows what is good and what is bad?"

The next day some thieves come and steal his valuable animal. His neighbour comes to commiserate with him, but the old man replies, "Who knows what is good and what is bad?"

A few days later the spirited stallion escapes from the thieves and joins a herd of wild mares, leading them back to the farm. The neighbour calls to share the farmer's joy, but the farmer says, "Who knows what is good and what is bad?"

The following day, while trying to break in one of the mares, the farmer's son is thrown and fractures his leg. The neighbour calls to share the farmer's sorrow, but the old man's attitude remains the same as before.

The following week the army passes by, forcibly conscripting soldiers for the war, but they do not take the farmer's son because he cannot walk. The neighbour thinks to himself, "Who knows what *is good and what is bad?"* and realises that the old farmer must be *a Taoist sage.*

From "The Tao Book and Card Pack" by Timothy Freke

This book started out describing to you what I thought was the worst day of my life. Which parlayed itself into a two-year downward spiral that almost destroyed me. But, I survived. And because I got help from many people along the way, I have grown and thrived over the last twenty years. I learned that if I walk through the fear, ask for help and take action, I can make any of my dreams come true. I've traveled abroad, owned my dream car, remarried and became a stepmom. I learned how to ride a motorcycle, and have gone skydiving. I became a grandma. I found my passion and started my own business. And, I've written this book! Now I want to pass that spirit, hope and motivation onto you!

We support each other in the recovery community. We understand each other when no one else can. We build each other up. We hold each other up. We do it one day at a time. Sometimes one hour or one minute at a time. We learn not to give in to our old behaviors. This involves a change in our thinking, developing a "Can Do" attitude, and a faith in a Higher Power. We work on our character defects. We try to remain humble and admit when we are wrong. We adopt an attitude of gratitude for the little things in life which we see as miracles.

If you have been in debt and climbed out of that valley, you can extend your hand and help someone else climb out as well. It is easier for them to climb up and out while someone is pulling them along as opposed to struggling to climb out. It is the same with grief, alcoholism, addiction, gambling, over-eating, shopping/acquiring, and for some people disorganization or clutter. This is what peer support provides.

You find somebody who has been through what you are going through and you find out how they did it. If someone helps you through it, you turn around and help the next person get through it. Get a mentor, be a mentor. Emulate those you admire. Attend a grief sharing meeting.

Another quote from Ruth Sissom's book *Moving Beyond Grief* is: "The pain of loss is always traumatic. But as our emotional trauma begins to subside, we can help to heal our own grief by reaching out with compassion and kindness to others who are hurting."

Many people go through a hardship and it inspires them to start a charity, a foundation, go into that field as a career, speak on the topic, or organize a fundraiser. Here are a few examples.

In 1935, a stockbroker was struggling to stay sober. He was away on business and tempted to go into the hotel lounge. Instead, he made a call to find out if anyone else in this town could put him in touch with someone who had his same struggle. He was introduced to a local doctor who was suffering badly from his own alcoholism. They met and talked one alcoholic to another. The stockbroker stayed sober and the doctor quit drinking. This was the beginning of the movement known as Alcoholics Anonymous. By 1939, the first 100 members helped shape the organization, by drafting the twelve steps, developing the twelve traditions, and wrote the book "Alcoholics Anonymous". This became the model of all other 12-Step recovery programs.

Nancy Goodman Brinker's only sister died from breast cancer in 1980 at the age of 36. She founded Susan G. Komen for the Cure® in 1982. In 1983, she founded the Susan G. Komen Race for the Cure® series, which is now the world's largest and most successful education and fundraising event for breast cancer. In 2010, Brinker released her New York Times best-selling memoir "Promise Me," an inspirational story of her transformation from bereaved sister to the undisputed leader of the ongoing international movement to end breast cancer. Today Ms. Brinker is the Founder and Chair of Global Strategy of Susan G. Komen. Now we have National Breast Cancer Awareness Month each October.

Milton Hershey failed at owning not one but two candy stores before he built the successful Lancaster Caramel Company. While his caramel business boomed, Hershey started the Hershey Chocolate Company. Hershey was determined to find a new formula that would allow him to mass-produce and mass-distribute milk chocolate candy. As the company grew and Hershey's wealth expanded, so did his philanthropy. Unable to have children of their own, the Hershey's focused a good portion of their giving on endeavors that affected kids. In 1909 the couple opened the Hershey Industrial School, a facility for orphaned boys. It has since become a landing spot for girls as well and is now known as the Milton Hershey School.

Who knows what is good and what is bad? They say hindsight is 50/50, meaning we see clearly when we look back at our lives. Tragedies can produce a wellspring of positive ripples. A simple idea to help someone other than ourselves can benefit millions around the globe. You never know how you may impact another person's life if you just take the action, or persevere through the heartaches. My hope is, after you finish reading this book, that you reread the pertinent sections of this book. Highlight sentences and phrases that speak to you. Make copies of the pages that have samples, tips, habits and motivations, and post them somewhere prominent in your home where you will see them and read them often. Re-evaluate your goals periodically. Use the book as a resource to refer back to time and again.

In doing this, I hope you will have the courage to change. Once you change, pass it on by helping someone else.

The delicate balance of mentoring someone is
not creating them in our own image, but giving
them the opportunity to create themselves.

– STEVEN SPIELBERG

Bibliography

How to Start a Home-Based Professional Organizing Business, by Dawn Noble. Secord Edition, Copyright © 2011 Morris Book Publishing, LLC.

Helping the Grieving Client, Institute for Challenging Disorganization, Publication No 18, written by Katherine D. Anderson, CPO-CD®, Copyright © 2004

20 Tips for Good Grieving, The Good Grief Center for Bereavement Support (GGC), a nonprofit charitable organization. Located at 2717 Murray Ave., Pittsburgh PA 15217-2419, 412-224-4700, or 1-888-474-3388, www.goodgriefcenter.com.

When Bad Things Happen to Good People, by Harold S. Kushner, Copyright © 1981 by Harold Kushner. Avon Books, An Imprint of Harper-Collins Publishers, 10 East 53rd Street, New York, NY 10022-5299. Published by arrangements with Schocken Books, Inc.

How to Write a Book in a Weekend; Author Starter Kit, Declaration of Author Intention, by Donna Kosik, www.writewithdonna.com, © 2012-2014 DONNA KOSIK

Andrew Gold, *Thank You For Being a Friend.* ©2016 Songfacts®, LLC. http://www.songfacts.com/detail.php?id=3386. July 27, 2016

Buried in Treasures: Help for Compulsive Acquiring, Saving, and Hoarding, by David F. Tolin, Randy O. Frost, Gail Steketee. First Edition, Oxford University Press 2007.

Smart Goals Guide. What Is A Smart Goal? Copyright 2010-2016. http://www.smart-goals-guide.com/smart-goal.html. July 27, 2016

Reverso, Dictionary, Collins English Dictionary 5th Edition first published in 2000. ©2016Reverso-SoftissimoSpiritual definition: http://dictionary.reverso.net/english-definition/spiritual%20 adviser. July 27, 2016

Susan G. Komen ©2016, Nancy G. Brinker Bio http://ww5.komen.org/AboutUs/NancyBrinker.html#sthash.YmPxNW8V.dpuf. July 27, 2016

Bio. Milton Hershey. © Bio and the Bio logo are registered trademarks of A&E Television Network, LLC. http://www.biography.com/people/milton-hershey-9337133. July 27, 2016

Moving Beyond Grief, Lessons From Those Who Have Lived Through Sorrow, by Ruth Sissom. Discovery House Publishers, Box 3566 Grand Rapids MI 49501. Copyright 1994 by Ruth M. Sissom

Two Big Myths about Grief, By Hal Arkowitz, Scott O. Lilienfeld on November 1, 2011. © *2016 Scientific American, a Division of Nature America, Inc.*
http://www.scientificamerican.com/article/grief-without-tears/ August 24, 2016

How Grief Works, by Alia Hoyt
How Stuff Works Science
http://science.howstuffworks.com/life/grief2.htm

Copyright © 2016 HowStuffWorks, a division of InfoSpace Holdings LLC
August 24, 2016

Healing Your Grieving Body: Physical Practices for Mourners, by Alan D. Wolfelt
Ph.D. Copyright 2007-2013, Center for Loss and Life Transition
http://griefwords.com/index.cgi?action=page&page=articles%2Fhealing_body.html&site_id=2
August 24, 2016

Your Health and Grief, By Tom Gray
Gray, T. (2016). Psych Central.
http://psychcentral.com/lib/your-health-and-grief/
Last reviewed: By John M. Grohol, Psy.D. on 17 Jul 2016
Originally published on PsychCentral.com on 17 May 2016. All rights reserved.
August 24, 2016

Health Matters With Dr. Sanjay Gupta
How Grief Can Make You Sick, By Dr. Sanjay Gupta
http://www.everydayhealth.com/news/how-grief-can-make-you-sick/
Copyright © 2016 Everyday Health Media, LLC
August 24, 2016

How does grief cause physical pain? By Jon Kelly
BBC News Magazine, 6 May 2016
http://www.bbc.com/news/magazine-36213249
August 24, 2016

Understanding Your Client: Grief and Loss presentation to NAPO Pittsburgh 8/5/2016 by Ellen Frese-March, MSCP, LPC, NCC, CCTP
Licensed Professional Counselor Psychotherapist
Orenda Counseling Center, LLC
Orendacc.com
Efm.orenda@gmail.com
412-406-7139

Neurological Aspects of Grief

Adriana C. Silva, Natalie P. De Olivira Ribeiro, Alexandre R. De Mello Schier, Oscar Arias-*Carrión,* Flavia Paes, Antonio E. Nardi, Sergio Machado and Tamires M. Pessoa

Article (PDF Available) in CNS & Neurological Disorders-Drug Targets (Formerly Current Drug Targets - CNS & Neurological Disorders) 13 (6); 930-6. August 2014

CNS & Neurological Disorders – Drug Targets, 2014, 13, 930-936
©2014 Bentham Science Publishers
https://www.researchgate.net/publication/263096191_Neurological_Aspects_of_Grief

Appendix A:

PHILOSOPHIES

Philosophy #1: If you don't talk to yourself with respect, how can you expect anyone else to?

Philosophy #2: Walk through your fear.

Philosophy #3: Anything is possible, if you put your mind to it.

Philosophy #4: Sometimes things happen for a reason.

Philosophy #5: Unanswered prayers (or failures) can be a blessing in disguise.

Philosophy #6: Build relationships with people who you can help and who can help you.

Philosophy #7: There, but for the Grace of God, go I.

Appendix B:

RESOURCES

National Association of Professional Organizers, http://www.napo.net/
1120 Rt 73, Suite 200 • Mount Laurel, NJ 08054 • 856.380.6828 • Fax: 856.439.0525

Institute of Challenging Disorganization http://challengingdisorganization.org/
ICD 1693 S. Hanley Rd. St. Louis, MO 63144 -- 314-416-2236

Clutterers Anonymous, http://clutterersanonymous.org/contact-us/
Phone: To leave a voice message for CLA, call CLA WSO at 866-402-6685. A volunteer will return your call.
Mail: Clutterers Anonymous World Service Organization (CLA WSO)
PO Box 91413
Los Angeles, CA 90009-1413

MADD, Mothers Against Drunk Drivers, http://www.madd.org/
MADD National Office
511 E. John Carpenter Freeway, Suite 700
Irving, TX 75062
Phone: 877.ASK.MADD or 877.275.6233
Fax: 972-869-2206/07

Lisa Purk, Life Coach
Inner Fire
lisa@fuelyourinnerfire.com
412-997-7215

Stephanie Scanlon, Owner/Principle Decorator
Decorating Den Interiors
http://stephaniescanlon.decoratingden.com/
412-464-9655

Dan Hudock, Sandler Training, http://www.dan.sandler.com/
115 VIP Drive, Suite 210
Wexford, PA 15090
dan@sandler.com
724-940-2388

About the Author

*T*his is Dorothy Clear's first book. She earned a Bachelor's degree in business administration from Robert Morris College. She had a 23 year career in corporate environments covering human resource, safety and worker's compensation. Then, in September 2011 she established her own company Clear Organization.

In addition to adding author to her list of roles, she is a career woman, entrepreneur, wife, mom, stepmom, grandma, motorcyclist, gardener and mentor.

She is a member of the National Association of Professional Organizers (NAPO). She is also an active member of the NAPO - Pittsburgh chapter, where she has served as director of marketing, board secretary, and two-term president.

She is involved with the Hoarding Task Force in Allegheny County (Pittsburgh, PA, her home town). She is one of four founding core members who have initiated a hoarding task force in neighboring Beaver County where she currently lives.

She is a member of the Beaver County Chamber of Commerce; teaches non-credit courses on organizing at local community colleges, senior centers and residential facilities; and loves public speaking.

She has been quoted in the Pittsburgh Post-Gazette, Beaver County Times, and North Hills Monthly Magazine, interviewed on KDKA radio, and worked on an episode of the A&E show <u>Hoarders</u>.

Ideals Dorothy lives by:

- Life is good at any age.
- Don't stay stuck in your life.
- Follow your passion.
- Pray daily.
- To thine own self be true.

May 2017
- Prayer time upon arising - denning
  + some personal Reading   Room

- fix breakfast
- dress for the day
- check 3 today items
   Begin -

- Y - water aerobics 3x a week